Get a G.R.I.P. on Presentations:
Andrew's Ax Semi-Secret Guide on
What to Say and How to Say It

ALSO BY ANDREW W. SILBERMAN

Get a G.R.I.P. - Andrew's Ax Guide to Global Readiness ®

First edition, March 2012. Second edition, July 2017.

Get a G.R.I.P. on Presentations:
Andrew's Ax Semi-Secret Guide on
What to Say and How to Say It

Andrew W. Silberman

Enlightening Press

Copyright to the first edition, 2019 by Andrew W. Silberman.

This edition was published by Enlightening Press.

All rights reserved. No part of this book may be reproduced, stored in a retrieval system, or transmitted in any form or by any means, electronic, mechanical, photocopying, recording, or otherwise, without the written permission of the publisher.

Cover designed by www.rehderandcompanie.com

CONTENTS

Testimonials ix
Preface xv
Introduction xxi
The 3 Vs xxvii

Chapter 1 | 1
Chapter 2 | 9
Chapter 3 | 19
Overcoming Common Obstacles to Great Presentations | 27
Chapter 4 | 28
Chapter 5 | 33
Chapter 6 | 38
Chapter 7 | 43
Questions and Answers | 46

References 53
If You Enjoyed This Book... 55
About the Author 57

TESTIMONIALS

"Every leader realizes their greatest opportunity to lead is while on stage addressing employees, customers, partners, or investors. Yet few leaders really appreciate or understand how to make the most of these opportunities and truly excel. *G.R.I.P.* is the best formula available to make the most of every opportunity to be a world class presenter, communicator, and leader. I realize this after 30 years of best effort, mistake-filled presentations, and wish I had access to *G.R.I.P.* much earlier in my career. I and all future leaders will be well-served by this book."

—Tom Reilly, Former CEO of Cloudera (NYSE:CLDR), ArcSight (NASDAQ: ARST), and Trigo Technologies (Acquired by IBM)

"Get a G.R.I.P. on Presentations is a must read if you're

ready to take your speaking and presentation skills to the next level. Andrew authentically shares his best practices from his hard won experience as a coach, speaker and game changer. This book will get you excited to be in front of any group, big or small, with the confidence and clarity it takes to inspire."

—Devon Bandison, Author "Fatherhood Is Leadership: Your Playbook for Success, Self-Leadership and a Richer Life"

"*Get a G.R.I.P. on Presentations* encapsulates succinctly Andrew Silberman's unique gifts he offers others in preparing for public presentations, whatever the context or size of audience. Having known Andrew as a fellow member of the American Chamber of Commerce in Japan for many years, our experiences in the business world could not have been more different. My decades as a lawyer in the corporate world, with both U.S. and Japanese companies in Japan, had made me confident in addressing business audiences using PowerPoint slides, with a certain speed and content, designed to be effective with a mixture of English and non-English speakers. Andrew's experience, cultivated through years as a successful entrepreneur working with business people of varied backgrounds, brings a whole different perspective, with a focus on making you effective with particular audiences, based on who you really are, reflected in your body language and tone. The lessons I have learned, including building self-confidence, using good humor, and exhibiting human empathy, while working with him in my efforts to become an effective leader at the ACCJ, have proven invaluable throughout my career and I continue to implement the lessons he shares in this guide to this day."

—Larry Bates, Board Member and General Counsel, Panasonic Corporation, President, American Chamber of Commerce in Japan 2013

"Having heard Andrew present on presenting, having read other presenting guides, and having watched a number of videos in the subject, I thought I knew all there was to know about the topic. Yet, Andrew's latest "*Get a G.R.I.P*" not only helpfully summarized everything I already knew, it also included a number of points I didn't, as well as directions to further useful resources. And all in a manageable, easy-to-absorb, size. I'll certainly be keeping my copy on hand for future presentations, as well as recommending for my colleagues."

—Ryann Thomas, Partner, PwC Tax Japan, Vice President, American Chamber of Commerce in Japan (ACCJ)

"I ain't got time for that!" That's the first thing that came to mind when Andrew Silberman asked me to read his new book, "*Get a G.R.I.P. on Presentations*."

Those six words also spew from my mouth every time Andrew assigns me anything that seems time-consuming or repetitive as my executive communication coach. Most of us are "busy" with work or other activities we feel out-prioritize things we really aren't interested in doing. However, I felt I owed it to Andrew to read his new book and to let him know what I think. Surprisingly, I finished it in my spare time over a couple of days and found the material extremely valuable for anyone wanting to improve their presentation skills. Andrew has taken what he has shared with me over the years as my coach and summed it up in a very concise and easy-to-read book. Everything from the "Three Vs" to the "Three Ps" are concepts he has shared with me over the years to help me become a better presenter, and my colleagues have told me that I am better. The hard part is putting everything into practice, and practice is something we should all do to become better. I have another presentation coming up this week and reading the book has reminded me of the things I ought to be doing to shine. *"Get a G.R.I.P. on Presentations"* is an invaluable reference for anyone with a desire to improve on presentations.

—James Webb, Director of Information Technology, North Asia for a Global Manufacturing Company

"Get a G.R.I.P. on Presentations is the next step in your

evolution as a public speaker. Not only do I use *Get a G.R.I.P.* for my personal growth, I use it to educate all of SPHER's staff members in addition to training our summer interns so they gain an understanding of Andrew's core teachings. AMT, Andrew and the *Get a G.R.I.P* series play an integral part of the SPHER, Inc. corporate culture."

—Ray Ribble, CEO, SPHER (Los Angeles, CA)

"*Get a G.R.I.P.* is a must-read for global leaders, a fresh 'how-to' for effective presentations."

—Paul DuPuis, Managing Director & CEO, Randstad India

"This book is easy to read and Andrew hits the points about "presentations." I have done presentations over 10 years for people interested in our graduate business program. Yet, I have always asked how I can present better so that my message will get to the audience's heart and be remembered? Andrew's advice in the book is valuable because it works for presenting to both global and Japanese-only audiences. I improved my presentation greatly!"

—Dr. Mikiya Mori, Director, Executive MBA Program, Temple University Japan Campus

PREFACE

Get a G.R.I.P. ® on Presentations: Andrew's Ax Semi-Secret Guide on What to Say and How to Say It

First, the facts or the FAQs:

Q1. Isn't that a presumptuous title? You're going to *tell me* what to say and how to say it?

A1. Yes, it is. And yes, I am. Sort of. I'm going to *suggest* what to say and how to say it *for your maximum impact*. I'm going to help you create and deliver presentations that your audiences can follow, understand, and remember. You don't need to trust me; just test the ideas. Keep what works and throw out what doesn't.

Q2. Are you really going to divulge your secrets here? Won't this take away from your coaching and training practice?

A2. First, there are no "secrets" when it comes to creating and delivering excellent presentations. All that I cover in this book, in my workshops, and with my coaching clients is widely known; it's just that what's known isn't being widely applied. As the phrase goes, "Common sense is not common practice." Even after reading this book and nodding along (hopefully not nodding off!), clients will come into my office to practice an important speech and, together, we'll find five or more things he or she can improve.

I played competitive tennis and later coached for a few years. You can't learn to play tennis from a book. If you want to improve your tennis, Tim Gallwey's *Inner Game* series and Vic Braden's videos will complement lessons and practices. Books, magazine articles, and videos–they all helped my game. So the bigger "danger" comes from readers who *think* they now have presentations all figured out. I wrote this book, and I have coached over 1,000 business people on how to improve their presentation impact, and, still, I am learning every day. There's always more to explore.

Q3. If there's nothing really "new," then why write this book at all? Can't you just recommend the best that's out there?

A3. Yes, I can (and do) recommend the best materials that I have come across so far. (See the reference section at the end of the book.) And if you take the time, you can read or listen to the books, and watch the videos yourself and you will raise your skills. However, all that takes time. This little guide can save you that time. It's a curated version of some of the best ideas I've seen and heard, filtered through my subjective point of view. The most important learning will take place when you attend and deliver more presentations. After digesting this guide, you will be more attuned to what works and what doesn't work for you and for others. You'll be better at presenting yourself, and you'll be able to offer better advice to colleagues who are open to improvement.

Q4. Do these tips, tricks, techniques, or whatever you call them, work across cultures?

A4. Yes and no. Human beings communicate using the three Vs: Verbal, Vocal, and Visual elements covered in this guide. Different cultures, same three Vs. However, the specifics of exactly what *kind* of words, what *type* of sounds, and which specific visual elements work (or hurt) differ greatly across countries, companies, and situations, hence the term "Audience Analysis."

Who is your primary audience? What's the situation? How can you meet or exceed their expectations? These are questions to ask before each and every presentation. As any professional stand-up comic will tell you: the same joke that bombs in one setting can soar in another.

Q5. What's the biggest obstacle to becoming a great presenter?

A5. I'd rather share the best way to become a better presenter. I see three keys: 1) Seek instruction—from books like this, articles, videos, coaches, etc.; 2) Be open to feedback–from camera replays, from your audiences, from coaches, etc.; 3) Remember that practice makes progress. Presentations are major aspects of professional life that you can definitely take to the next level, no matter where you stand today.

Q6. Is this your final word on presentations?

A6. Not at all. I'm asking you, dear reader, to please send me feedback or questions related to the three Vs. Write me at andrew@amt-group.com. I will answer you personally and, if your question is "good enough," I'll include it (with credit to you, if you wish) in the next edition of this book. That's the beauty of working with Enlightening Press—a new edition can come out in just a couple of months.

And speaking of good or good-enough questions, I want to quote a favorite line from a fantastic resource. This comes from Jay Sullivan, author of *Simply Said: Communicating Better at Work and Beyond.* Jay writes, "We all learned in grade school that there are no stupid questions. And we all learned from business meetings that there are a lot of stupid questions." Have no fear: I won't expose your stupid questions, but I will promote your good ones!

INTRODUCTION

"Here's an amazing finding: Of the total impact of your presentation, only 7% is determined by the words you use, 38% is determined by the tone of your voice, and 55% by your nonverbal communications. (Source: Professor Albert Mehrabian, U.C.L.A.)"

I first read those words, including the source, in 1994 in David Peoples' excellent, now out-of-print book, *Presentations Plus*. I took those words to heart and on to our clients. Mr. Peoples dedicated the next few pages of his book to "Nonverbal Communications," and we created some exercises and borrowed some of his points to make the case for engaging the audience nonverbally.

Later in the 1990s and into the early 2000s, a controversy developed over Mehrabian's research, with some critics going so far as to label it "ridiculous on its face," asking, for example, how someone could communicate the above "amazing finding" without using words, or asking, in another example, if "Mehrabian's rule means there's not much lost meaning even if you don't speak the same language as the presenter."

This was pre-Twitter, so due to some good blog posts, along with Mehrabian's website explanation, the controversy died down rather than explode, but something was lost. The genius of Mehrabian's research was not in determining precisely what percentage of "liking" is determined by which of three modes of communicating, even though that's what his limited research concluded. Rather, the genius was in highlighting and bringing to public attention the three communication modes: Verbal, Vocal, and Visual.

Why is this even more important than Mehrabian's conclusions and the controversy that followed? Because even if the results had been different; say that each of the three Vs was equally important, or one of the other two Vs was more impactful than Visual, Mehrabian reminds us that we, as presenters, have only three ingredients at our disposal in order to impress, inspire, or inform our audience: we have 1) the words our audience processes, 2) the tone of voice our audience hears, and 3) whatever we put into the audience's field of vision.

That's why "The Three Vs" is my favorite topic,

whether I'm speaking to a group or coaching an individual on presentations, leadership, negotiations, meetings, teleconferences, teambuilding, and even listening skills. All of these are subsets of "communication," and all can fall under the umbrella of "The Three Vs."

Hence, this presumptuous little guidebook. I've culled 25+ years of my own investigations into what makes better presentations, along with well over 10,000 hours coaching (often "fighting with") business executives on how to increase their impact. I still remember the time, back in the early 1990s, when executives from Exxon informed me that their corporate rules stated that all the OHPs (remember them? "Overhead Projector Slides") contain only black and white text, in ALL CAPS. I was minutes away from delivering a workshop to them. I told the training manager that I would need to change the name of the workshop from "Effective Presentations" to "Ineffective Presentations."

This book can be taken as "notes from the field," and is from and for all those executives as much as it is from and for me. That's part of the reason it's so short. Businesspeople are busy people. Mark Twain (and Blaise Pascale, too) have been quoted as writing, "I'm sorry this letter is so long. I didn't have time to make it shorter." I am taking time to make this as short as I can while still covering most of the basics, and some of what's too often missed, related to the three Vs. I hope you'll be reminded of something that inspires improvement in your next presentation or that helps you spot what someone does particularly well or poor next time, so that, again, you can improve or help them improve.

Warning: Read at Your Own Risk

I sometimes open workshops with a picture of a beautiful, giant tree. I then introduce the biblical story of creation, including the Tree, and ask, "What is this tree?" Western audiences generally know it as "The Tree of Knowledge." But its complete name is "The Tree of Knowledge of Good and Evil." I remind the audience that after eating the fruit of that tree, God kicked Adam and Eve out of the Garden. Paradise (and innocence) lost.

After reading the pages of this book, you too will have consumed the fruit of knowledge of good and evil, or at least good and bad presentations. For better and for worse, you're going to know why some presentations soar and others suck. It's then going to be obviously, clearly, up to you to determine which type of presenter you want to be.

I LOVE great presentations about as much as I HATE bad ones. After you've read this book, you'll have no excuse for delivering (or allowing, if you're in charge) a bad presentation to go forward. You may not always get to "great" but you will at least get to "good," or at least beyond "Death by PowerPoint," which is a big step in the right direction.

One last thought before we dive in. Having grown up in California, I toyed for a while with a fourth "V." What about "Vibe?" I thought. But then I realized even "Vibe" reflects how someone looks and sounds, how they carry themselves. But I decided "Vibe" deserves a little more attention. So I devote the first chapter of the second section to overcoming a lack of "presence." More Presence = Better Vibe.

The book is divided into two parts. Part I is your Breakfast, Lunch, and Dinner, i.e. the three Vs: The Verbal, Vocal, and Visual elements of a presentation. Part II is a dessert sampler. Those of us watching our weight usually avoid dessert, and these three chapters discuss obstacles to avoid or overcome: lack of presence, lack of preparation & practice, and what to do about boring topics.

Hopefully, this'll be a quick, enjoyable read, and you'll find something to implement in your next presentation. And be inspired to look in and around for more ways to improve. We're all on this tiny speck of dust, spinning on its own axis, hurtling through a vast universe of mostly empty space. It's up to us to put some meaning and entertainment into our limited time here together.

THE 3 VS

1

"Poets, priests, and politicians have words to thank for their positions." — opening lyrics from the song, "De Do Do Do De Da Da Da."
– Gordon Summer (Sting), recorded by the Police

VERBAL: Getting a G.R.I.P. on What to Say

The quote above applies to every presenter. We start with what you say, because that's where most of us spend most of our time in preparation and focus. The simple truth is this: You're on stage (or at the table, or across the desk) because of *words*. So despite the greater relative vocal and visual impact on your audiences, words do matter. A lot. It would hardly make sense to practice visual gestures and vocal variation with a bunch of gibberish when you have something meaningful to get across.

S.U.C.C.E.S.

A WHOLE BOOK could be written on the verbal portion of your presentation alone. In fact, an excellent one already was, by Chip and Dan Heath: *Made to Stick: Why Some Ideas Survive and Others Die.* We summarize their "Six Elements" in our coaching and workshops for one reason: they work. You can read their book, listen to Chip Heath's keynote on YouTube, or watch or read one of several book summaries online.

The reason I quote the Heath brothers here and recommend their book so strongly is that *Made to Stick* inspired me to change a lot about how we teach and coach presentations. They make an impeccable argument (with statistics to back it up) that in order to have people remember your presentation, content really does matter.

As a reminder (or introduction for some of you), the 6 elements of S.U.C.C.E.S. are "Simple," "Unexpected," "Credible," "Concrete," "Emotional," and "Story." The more of these 6 elements you include in what you say, the more likely your message will get through to your audience and "stick" in their memories.

A little more on "Simple." You may have heard of the acronym "K.I.S.S." ("Keep It Short & Simple" or, more crudely, "Keep It Simple Stupid!") In their book, the Heath brothers detail both *why* it's important to keep your message simple and also how difficult it can be to do so. A great way to discover if your message is "simple" enough is to ask a smart 12-year-old if he or she understands your main points. You might think you're being clear when you're not, as several of my clients have discovered, to their dismay, when I've brought a smart 12-year-old to sit in judgment.

I love the Heath brothers' take on the "Curse of Knowledge," and their many examples of both complex and then simplified messages. They also run you through exercises to rate the level of simplicity of a given message. We're not talking about "dumbing down," and we're not talking about accuracy either. Your speech need not be correct to be remembered. Anyone who saw or heard of the O.J. Simpson trial still remembers one line above all the rest: "If it doesn't fit, you must acquit." Simple. Memorable. In other words, "sticky." (And we conveniently forget or never learned that O.J. was advised to stop taking arthritis medicine right before the trial, causing "the Juice's" hands to swell up.)

Why is it difficult to simplify a message? Because

once you know something, it is hard, *very* hard, to remember what it felt like *before* you knew it. And this makes it doubly hard to communicate to someone who has not discovered what you now know. So first, think back, and as best you can, reconstruct your learning path toward what you want to share. Without going into too much detail, hit the highlights along the way.

Empathy, that is, being able to put yourself in your audience's shoes, will help you find that space between confusing and boring. If you assume your audience already knows something that they don't know, you'll confuse them. And if you assume they *don't* know something that they already *do* know, you run the risk of boring them. Only by studying and being in tune with the audience can you hit that spot between boring and confusing.

Find the sweet spot by introducing new concepts or ideas in logical steps, building on what the audience does already know or believe, and by sharing familiar concepts or ideas in a fresh, new way, with personal anecdotes or examples.

For details of the rest of their "S.U.C.C.E.S." formula, check out their book, online summaries, or keynote on YouTube. It'll be worth your time.

The ABCs and the Power of Three

. . .

How many chords are there in a classic blues song? How many lights are there on a traffic signal? How about medals are awarded for a given competition in the Olympics? What's going on here? Something in this Universe has decreed that, as the three-minute (!) Schoolhouse Rock song said: "Three is a Magic Number." Yes, it is.

So let's make some magic with the Number three. If you can, find a special kind of three, what I call a MECE (pronounced like "geese") Triad. "MECE" stands for "Mutually Exclusive Collectively Exhaustive" and "Triad" stands for three. If you can, narrow (or broaden) your topic to include everything that's important in three, non-overlapping points. The simplest MECE Triad is to take whatever you're talking about and break it into the past, present, and future of that topic. That MECE Triad works for just about everything. But if you use it every time you present, you'll remove the second of the Heath brother's S.U.C.C.E.S. elements, "Unexpected," so don't overuse Past/Present/Future. Just keep in mind that "time" can be one of the better ways to organize your topic into a simple MECE triad.

You've heard it said, "There's no time like the present," but there really is *no* way to divide the passage of time other than into present, past, and future. That's what makes time a perfect MECE Triad.

Note the word "point." To support your main

message, create and deliver three *points*. Not three phrases. Not three paragraphs. And certainly not three (or 33) text-filled PowerPoint slides. And, by the way, putting a bullet point (•) in front of a sentence does not magically turn the sentence into a point. A point is sharp. A point is short. You may need a lot of words, pictures, or graphs to illustrate or re-enforce your three points, but aim to boil down your message to points, in their simplest form. This naturally happens when you look for the MECE Triad points for certain subjects, for example:

PROJECTS:
　1) Time
　2) Quality
　3) Cost

FITNESS:
　1) Diet
　2) Exercise
　3) Sleep

PRESENTATIONS:
　1) Verbal
　2) Vocal
　3) Visual

. . .

EXTRA BONUS for you when you find a MECE triad that's also easy to remember, like when your main three points rhyme (the "three Vs"). Rhymes help memory. Or when the first letter of each point could become an easy-to-remember acronym. A client found it easier for the team to remember their five values by arranging the first letters in a certain order, which spelled out "BIRCH." Remembering "BIRCH" values was easier than remembering five separate words. So when their Country manager wanted to speak about 1) Values, 2) Where We Are Now, and 3) Where We Are Going, he could put a picture of a birch tree to spark their memories, and he turned five values into one simple BIRCH point.

Sometimes you can use the "ABCs" of your topic. Have you noticed that we all learn the ABCs, and not the ABs nor the ABCDs? Why is that? As Jim Rohn was prone to saying: "I don't know. You don't know. Nobody knows." But it's a guideline that's been tried, tested, and true (a "Three T" triad), so: "Fly with the geese, use MECE!"

Two more MECE triad example questions I like to share with my classes and clients, and both answers are a "BLD" triad. How many meals do most of us eat in a day? (Spanish audiences will say "five," but let's leave flamenco out of this.) Three, right? Breakfast, Lunch, and Dinner. BLD. Maybe that's because, "What's common to all living things on Earth?" Again, BLD. We're Born, we Live, and we....

If you combine the Power of Three with the Heath brothers' S.U.C.C.E.S. formula, then at least the verbal component of your presentation will not "Die."

2

"And the vision that was planted in my brain still remains, within the sound of silence."
-- Paul Simon, "The Sound of Silence," performed by Simon & Garfunkel

VOCAL: Getting a G.R.I.P. on How to Say It

As you'll recall from the introduction, how you sound can make up 38% of the impact of your presentation. For the mathematically challenged (or inclined) that's over five times more impact than your words themselves. Even if you don't fully accept Mehrabian's conclusions, you know instinctively that how you say something affects others more than your words themselves. Need convincing? Can you, by changing just the tone of your voice, communicate the very *opposite* of the words you say? You can, right? When a fan says, "Oh, yeah, that referee's call was *really* fair," you can tell by the tone of their voice if the fan thinks the call was *un*fair. So listen in to your vocal quality, and check to see that what's intended is being communicated. And remember, it's your audience, not you, who determines whether or not you communicated clearly.

And consider this: If someone can't hear you, how can what you say matter at all? Imagine that a presenter announces from the stage: "Who would like to know the secret of getting any and everything you ever wanted in life?" Then he or she begins: "All you need is..." and then covers their mouth so that no one can hear the "secret."

In ancient history, Pericles said, "The thinking human being, not able to express himself, stands at the same level as those who cannot think." We can add or modify this to say, "The presenter, not heard, stands at the same level as those who cannot present."

It's not what you say. It's what your audience *hears* that counts. So let's focus some extra effort on how we sound.

(SOME OF THE following are an edited version of chapter 21 from *Get a G.R.I.P.: Andrew's Ax Guide to Global Readiness* ®.)

. . .

"You're talking a lot, but you're not saying anything." David Byrne, Psycho Killer, performed by the Talking Heads

I play rhythm guitar and sing lead vocal for Moonshots. There are more parallels than you might expect between playing in a band and working within any professional organization. One is the importance of recording what you do.

Turn on the Recorder

Our lead guitarist records all of our practice and live sessions on a digital recorder. He says this is the best, or perhaps the only way to figure out the places you need to work on. You might think a song sounded great, but until you've listened to it after you've played, until you've heard it the way your audience did, you don't really know.

It's best to practice your presentation in front of a live audience---family members will do---along with a video camera. For better or for worse, your camera will never walk out on you. It may be painful to watch and listen to yourself, but the rewards are huge. After recording your presentation, review it for the three Vs. Ideally, take time to watch three times: once for the verbal content; once for the visual; and then once, close your eyes and just listen to how you sound.

A professional coach can point out patterns or specific language that helps or hurts communication without a recording. But seeing and hearing yourself in action will leave a more lasting impression on the person most interested in your improvement: YOU.

After listening to yourself, decide what you want to improve. When we're nervous, our breathing gets shallower. Guess what happens to our vocal presentation? We speed up, and our pitch rises. After you listen to your own voice, ask yourself if you want it to be higher, lower, faster, or slower About 80% of the time, my clients are aiming at lower and slower than their video shows them.

When you want to communicate passion, enthusiasm, or energy, speed up and raise your volume. But when you want to communicate thoughtfulness, thoroughness, or expertise, you're better off going "low and slow."

What if your voice sounds flat, if it's not "resonant?" Practice humming for five minutes every morning, and then after a month, see how much better your recorded voice sounds. There may not be a cure for the common cold, but there is a cure for a non-resonant voice: a simple hum! Who would have thought that Winnie-the-Pooh was *that* smart? And for those who really want to dive into this, check out Per Bristow's "The Singing Zone." Per turns average Joes into rock stars and sends rock stars' voices into orbit.

Pauses

If there is a "trick" to more impactful presentations, this may be it: pause. Pauses are the single biggest, overlooked, underused tool in your kit. Pauses can get rid of filler words like "um," "ah," "like," "you know," "basically," etc. When you replace those filler words (or, better said, "non-words") with pauses, you'll look and sound smarter. You can pause for emphasis before, or after, an important point to increase the impact of that point. Pause for dramatic effect. Pause to get people to listen more closely. Pause to refocus. Pause to gain and keep control of the floor. And here's the most important reason to pause:

See? You wanted to know, right? And that's why I call the pause a "trick." Even if you have nothing important to say, pausing at the right place will make it *seem* important. But when used properly, not as a trick, all the better. As Paul Simon sang, "The vision that was planted in my brain still remains, in the sound of silence." How much silence did you deliberately put into your last presentation? How about putting some into your next one?

Variety, the Spice of Life

Vocal variety is where you can bring what you're saying to life. Vary your speed, vary your tone, vary your volume and pitch for maximum impact. You want to avoid monotone (same root as "monotonous"), but don't get carried away into "sing-song voice." You have surely heard this advice before. You know it intuitively. Variety and pauses work. You know by watching good actors and presenters. But in *every* workshop where I give a simple script to read, even when we've intentionally left a double-length gap between paragraphs, people pause at *most* one second between those paragraphs. Participants are then shocked when I show the movie clip and we all see the actor pauses for 13 full seconds between the paragraphs.

In the same exercise, almost everyone raises their voice to emphasize a key point in the script, but in the movie scene, the actor *lowers* his voice to even greater effect. To be fair, people "fail" at the exercise because they don't have the actor's coaching. In this case, I'm not only referring to the coaching Robert

Redford received as a professional actor, but also to the coaching his character receives in the movie. The movie, "The Candidate," is all about a political campaign, and the plot includes the painstaking time the candidate character (Redford) invests honing his stump speech. The candidate tested the vocal elements as much as everything else, and you can almost picture him counting to himself in order to hold the 13 seconds of silence.

By the way, I am not suggesting you pause for 13 seconds during your next business presentation. Someone might call for an ambulance. But test how you sound with a few, carefully chosen dramatic pauses placed strategically throughout your presentation. The difference may astound you. And your audience.

Microphones

A COMMON QUESTION in my workshops and coaching practice is, "To mic or not to mic?" My answer is simple: If there are more than 20 people in the room, or more than a few rows deep, opt for the microphone. Many presenters make the mistake of thinking that if they have a strong-enough voice, there's no need for a mic. But increasing volume is only one purpose of a microphone. You don't use a mic *only* for those in the back to be able to hear you. I've seen speakers with booming voices ask if those in the back can hear. "YES!" the back row shouts, while those in the front row nearly cover their ears because the speaker's voice is so loud. A good microphone gives you more vocal variety options. For example, you can whisper and still be heard in the back of a room if a loudspeaker is carrying your voice. Many of you are old enough to remember one of the first MTV "Unplugged" sessions with Eric Clapton. If so, you may recall that even "unplugged," the man guitar fans called "God" used a microphone.

"But," you might be thinking, "without a mic, how can I do a 'mic drop?'" Let me take a stand here: I don't go for "mic drops" any more than I advocate tearing up your notes to show how you're now going to "speak from the heart." Both those gestures backfire more often than not. I'm offering tips, tricks, and techniques, not gimmicks.

Be sure to practice with the type of microphone that you will actually use and then check the mic at the venue to make sure it sounds good. A lapel mic is often most comfortable, but sometimes lapel mics sound awful. And if you then switch to a hand-held mic, but misuse it by waving it around or using it as a pointer, your vocal as well as visual impact suffers. Practice with the equipment you will use, get used to lots of different types of equipment, and be *ready*.

. . .

"But That's Not Me!"

When you listen to yourself, you might say, like most people in my workshops, "That's not my voice!" And guess what? You're right. The voice you hear through a device is not the same voice you hear between your ears. But here's the kicker: You are the only person on the planet who hears your own voice through the bones in your head. Everyone else hears your voice the way you sound on the recording, that voice that you are convinced "doesn't sound like me." As one good TEDx speaker said, your voice is a gift for others, not for you.

We conduct an experiment in my workshops and coaching that brings this point home, and also helps people improve their volume. You might try this now. Plug up your ears with your index fingers. Now, count to ten, starting from a very low volume at number 1, raising gradually the volume as you increase the number, rising to a peak at 10, then back down to 1. Note that to you, the volume doesn't change much, if at all. If you drop to a near whisper (but still with vocal tone), you can hear yourself just as clearly as you can at 10. The reason is, again, you are "hearing" through the bones in your jaw and head, not through your ears. In order to set an adequate volume, you need to know how *others* are hearing you.

It's not what you say, but how you sound, that makes a bigger impact. By working on your vocal quality, whether it's simply humming five minutes a day, watching YouTube videos on "vocal quality improvement," or taking Per's course, you will ensure that, like the old cartoon character Tennessee Tuxedo used to say, the vocal part of your presentation "will not fail!"

3

"I can see clearly now."
– Johnny Nash

VISUAL: Getting a G.R.I.P. on What Your Audience Sees

Now, we come face-to-face, or better said, eye-to-eye, with the biggest of the big three Vs: VISUAL, i.e. what your audience sees. This, according to Dr. Mehrabian, results in over half of your "likeability" as a speaker.

Pop quiz: If I were to ask you what your most recent audience "saw" throughout your presentation, an honest answer should probably be, "I'm not sure," "I don't know," or "My slides?" Why don't you know? Because if you're like most presenters, you're only rarely looking into the eyes of your audience as you speak. Now, occasionally, such as in a large, formal setting, stage lights prohibit you from looking into anyone's eyes. Even if you try, all you'll see are bright, blinding lights. In these rare instances, my advice is to fake it. Look out and around *as if* you are making eye contact. From the audience's perspective, your eyes will be connecting with theirs.

But most of us only rarely give presentations under those conditions. And yet, where are your eyes while giving your presentation? On your notes? Up in the air? At the screen behind you or the laptop in front of you? The only way to know for sure is if you've video-recorded your presentation. Watch and you may be surprised how often you are not directly connecting with someone in the audience.

Most presenters' eyes find their way anywhere except where they should be: making direct contact with an audience member. That was my biggest take away from Jay Sullivan's talk at the American Chamber of Commerce in Japan's workshop a few years ago. He said, "Every sound you make should be delivered to a pair of eyes."

By this, he explained, "Never speak with your eyes on their way down to your notes or a screen. Don't speak on the way up either." Maintain what Sullivan calls the "arc of silence." Stay quiet while your gaze shifts. Silence adds to your credibility and perceived thoughtfulness, and silence allows your audience to absorb what you're saying. If you look away from an audience member, connect immediately with another member.

When it comes to VISUAL impact, make sure your audience is seeing your eyes. Your eyes are your most important visual aid. "Windows to the soul" may be a cliché, but it may also be true. Different cultures have different norms related to appropriate eye contact. But when you're speaking to more than 10 or so people in the room, making a series of 5-10 seconds' worth of eye contact with each person, it will not be "too much." And do make sure to "spread the love." So many presenters who start off well, avoiding the "screen magnet," still make the mistake of focusing only on one or two key people, or one side of the room, and leaving others to their lonesome selves.

What Should I Do with My Hands?

So, eyes first. Next: hands. One of my favorite TEDx Talks is given by Allan Pease at Macquarie University. Go check it out. In sum, we have one of three natural ways of using our hands: open palm, closed palm, and pointing. The open palm gestures bring your audience into your world, the closed palm commands attention, and pointing is, just like grandma said, best to be avoided. First, like in everything else we've covered, comes self-awareness. Watch yourself on video and note where your hands are or are not moving.

You'll learn more about the impact of the three main gestures and other tidbits of knowledge and comedy Mr. Pease delivers. In addition to what he covers, I'll add that there are way more things people do "wrong" with their hands than what they do "right." If you're stuck with what to do, just keep them in the martial arts ready position, with one hand gently grasping the other at the wrist.

Other "wrong" (or rather, less effective, less impactful) gestures include the prayer pose, the professorial hands-behind-the-back, the drooping shoulder hand or hands in pocket, and probably the worst, folded arms. None of these present you as someone connecting with the audience.

Remember that when you do gesture, you need to take the audience's perspective. When you go from "left to right" or "west to east," make sure to move your hand the opposite way from your point of view. If charting an "increase" in sales, for example, start down to your right, and sweeps up to the left; that way, the audience will see the increase as they would if looking at a slide.

Speaking of slides, let's go a little deeper on these most commonly used visual aids. Most slides would be more appropriately called "visual hindrances" or "visual obstacles." These "aids" move the audience's focus to a screen, and then often serve to confuse rather than clarify points. How? First, by flashing text up on a screen, a presenter is silently directing the audience to read....and yet, at the same time, he or she usually continues speaking–and speaking different words than are on the screen.

To demonstrate how ineffective this is, I do the following during my one-on-one sessions: I pick up a random book, ask my client to read a paragraph, and then I start speaking to him or her. They immediately stop reading. Then I say, "Oh, go ahead, keep reading, I'm going to quiz you on the content." They go back to reading, and I say, "But what's really important is the following..." Their eyes pop back up to mine. That's usually the most it takes for the message to sink in. It is impossible to read and listen at the same time with anywhere near 100% comprehension of either input, let alone both.

And as Susan Weinschenk says in her 6-minute video, "5 Things Every Presenter Needs to Know About People," the visual input trumps the audio: as soon as someone is reading what you've put up on a slide, they are not listening to you.

That's just the beginning, though. The real problem is *before* introducing the slide, or rather, before *not* introducing the slide. Most slides just pop up with no introduction at all, like the old slide shows your grandfather set up at family reunions or when sharing vacation memories. "Oh, here's where we had dinner the first night...." Instead, tell your audience what the "next slide" is going to be. And when the slide pops up, introduce it properly, like you would a friend. What's the slide's name? It should appear clearly at the top of the slide, with an attention-grabbing headline; for example, "Sales Increased 15%," not just "Revenue." And any graphs should be identified e.g.: "Here's a pie chart showing where our sales are coming from..." or "This is a bar graph where you see each of our offices and how far over or under their sales targets they are as of today."

How often have you heard, "This slide is a little hard to read," or "it's a bit complex, but....?" Stop it! Make the hard-to-read slide easy-to-read. The "complex slide?" Take the time to simplify it. That's your job as a presenter, as a communicator, as a professional.

A memorable "good example of a bad example" took place in my office. A speaker was delivering his draft presentation when his boss came in, a bit late. The boss stood at the back of the room, eyes squinting as he tried to make out what was on the slide being shown. All the while, the presenter was speaking. Now, we already know that if someone is reading a slide, they are not listening to you; but, what happens when someone is *trying* (and failing) to read while you're speaking? How much information is penetrating the audience then? Answer: Just about zero.

As Susan Weinschenk says, "Try putting your presentation together without any slides first and then decide if any of your points would be *enhanced* by a visual example or illustration." (See her wonderful 6-minute YouTube post, *5 Things Every Presenter Needs to Know About People,* for a few more pearls of wisdom.)

Of the three Vs, "Vocal" is the one where variety is best: changing volume, pace, length of pauses, tone (high and low), etc., all help. "Variety is the spice of life." For Verbal, and especially for Visual, the rule is: KEEP IT SIMPLE. No more eye charts, no more undecipherable graphs, and for your audience's sake, no more text-filled slides that belong in a handout, a read-ahead, or a leave-behind. OK, end of rant. At least until I see the next crappy slide, and I hope it's not yours!

See yourself from the audience's perspective. If it's not what you say, or how you sound, but what your audience sees that makes the biggest impact, take the time to practice and hone your VISUAL presence.

OVERCOMING COMMON OBSTACLES
TO GREAT PRESENTATIONS

4

"I felt the fear in my mouth, and it refused to talk." — John Dee Graham, *Big Sweet Life*

Lack of Presence (Edited and updated version of Chapter 29 in Get A G.R.I.P.)

Speaking of presence, the 44th President of the United States walked into the room with it. So did his ambassador to Japan. And the Dalai Lama. I was fortunate enough to see all three in person over the span of one month, and I witnessed it first-hand: unmistakable on-stage presence.

What gives these three public figures, and others who also have it, their commanding presence? It's not in their mode of delivery. President Obama read entirely from a prepared text. Ambassador John

Roos would often glance down at notes, and the Dalai Lama spoke entirely "off the cuff." Three very different deliveries.

And it's not in the topics they addressed either. Obama talked about Asia, Ambassador Roos about Obama, and the Dalai Lama talked mostly about China. I've worked with clients on thousands of presentations over the past 25+ years, and I promise you: no one topic lends itself to "presence" more than any other.

Like you, I've sat through presentations whose topic should have, and could have, had me on the edge of my seat, but instead, my mind wound up focused only on how to politely get out of the room.

So if it's not the delivery, and it's not the topic, what is it?

Dig Deep

THE ANSWER, like the answer to most deep questions, lies at the root. In this case, the root of the word "presence"–to be *present*. Each of the three speakers, and all speakers who have that intangible quality we call "presence," make it known in their own way that they are physically and mentally "there," *with* their audience.

The Dalai Lama did it by stopping and chatting

with anyone and everyone who caught his eye on his way to the podium. I had never seen someone take so long to get from the back to the front of the Foreign Correspondents' Club. The Ambassador connected by referring to his immediate surroundings (including his stoic body guard); and the President connected by waving to and acknowledging people from all over a packed Suntory Hall. None of the three began by looking down at their notes.

Looking down at your notes or laptop has the same effect as snuffing out a candle at the start of a dinner party. And how foolish does it look when someone is apparently checking their notes in order to read off their own name or topic of their presentation? Don't snuff out your presentation at the start; let your light shine!

What Creates Presence?

Let's explore two enhancers of your ability to be *present* when you pre*sent*: 1) confidence and 2) your "energy vector."

Let's start with confidence. Like most statespeople, all three of those speakers have been through enough scrutiny to command presence on any stage. They've been grilled by the press and by both friendly and hostile audiences. Surviving those fires has clearly raised their confidence level. And of all attributes required of an excellent speaker, the one that gives the most presence is, without a doubt, confidence. Obama, Roos, and the Dalai Lama are confident people. Are you? What can you do to raise your confidence?

Next comes another intangible: the energy vector. Every presentations coach will tell you that knowing your audience is crucial to delivering a great presentation. But knowing, analyzing, and preparing for a specific audience, while crucial for a deep connection, is not the same as focusing your energy on that audience in the moment.

Most presenters apparently focus about 20% of their energy on their audience (and only directly connect with even less than 20% of the people), and they then divide the rest of their energy between making sure they deliver their content correctly and wondering how they are appearing to the audience. Neither Obama, Roos, nor the Dalai Lama appeared overly focused on himself. In fact, I don't think the Dalai Lama had any focus at all on himself. Their energy vectors were directed outward, to and for their audiences.

Visual Aids?

. . .

NONE of these speakers used any kind of visual aid. They were their own visual aid. Why distract your audience with something on a screen? If you want presence, you need the audience's eyes on you, not the screen. And if you choose to put up a word or two, make it just that: a word or two at a time. Not ten. And certainly not sixty!

When you do use a slide to bring home a point, leave the slide up only as long as you are talking about it. When finished, "blank" the screen by hitting the "B" button on your keyboard or using the "blank" button on your portable slide changer. It's not a slide show; it's time for *you* to share what you know, how you think, what you feel.

It isn't the content of your slides that give you presence; rather, as Martin Luther King Jr. would say, it's the content of your character. That and the energy you project to and for your audience will help you increase the intangible that all great presenters have: presence. And the way you present presence is through a confident, masterful use of the three Vs.

5

Lack of Preparation & Passion (Edited, updated version of chapter 30 from *Get a G.R.I.P.*)

Following up on "Presence!" I'm going to share with you how two more Ps, "preparation" and "passion" affect speakers and audiences, and how proper preparation can overcome some overlooked obstacles to good public speaking.

Several years ago, I joined a seminar given by the University of Chicago's Booth School of Business. Here, I'll focus on the sessions featuring Mark Zmijewski, at the time acting Dean of the Booth business school, and professor Ron Burt.

SETTING the scene

. . .

The day got off to a happy start. I arrived with my colleague and we were greeted by Leslie Taylor, the Booth School's Assistant Director for Asia, who showed us into the seminar room and offered us a wide selection of muffins, bagels, sandwiches, and coffee. As the room filled, right on time, an associate dean introduced the Mark Zmijewski (hereafter referred to as he's known by colleagues, Mark Z).

It turns out that Mark Z has been connected to the University since 1984, and he knows the school about as well as anyone possibly could. He shared some interesting facts, including that John D. Rockefeller started the school with a private investment equivalent to $200 million in today's money. It was, according to the tycoon, "the best investment [he] ever made."

Technophobes rejoice!

Mark Z's purpose was to market the school. And while he performed well, his technology didn't. The PowerPoint slides kept failing to load properly, and no less than three people took turns to divine the reason and then to fix the problem. Once fixed,

Mark could get back to his talk. Until the next slide failed. Scramble. Fix. Fail. Repeat.

Now Mark Z is a big man (well over 6 feet and 250 pounds), and his presence and passion for the university are self-evident—the man commands attention.

But watching the crowd of helpers trying to get his slides to work was painful. First, we were wasting precious time. A whole slate of speakers was on board for this seminar. Who wants to sit through a long commercial, even if it's good? Second, the glitches made the Booth School or the hosting company, Black Rock, or both, look technically incompetent.

Third, and most important, the slides were unnecessary. They were black & white text-filled screen fillers that only detracted from Mark Z's powerful presence. Like some kids' tonsils, they had "joined the other side." Even when they were "working," they were hurting.

Lessons for Readers: If your next presentation contains slides like his, leave them home. And even if you have good slides, the ones that activate the right side of the brain, the ones that help make your message stick, then you *still* need to be ready to go it alone. That way, when the glitches come (and come they will), you can still win the day–if you're prepared.

. . .

Passion to the rescue

Next came Professor Ron Burt. He had provided us with his slides as handouts, and at first glance. I thought, "Oh no." Complex would be an understatement. Swirls of data points, dotted and solid lines between names, and lots of text. My colleague shrugged and asked, "Do you think we're going to be able to understand this?" I had my doubts.

But then the Professor began to speak. With passion. He referred us to the handouts with the promise that we would not only understand them, but that we would gain something valuable for our lives and for our businesses by doing so as well.

He focused on just one or two slides for the majority of his presentation. Actually, that's not true. He never focused on a slide. Even when he jogged up to the screen from the back of the room (the Professor made full use of the space around him), and pointed at a specific piece of data, his focus, meaning his attention, was always on us, not on his material. That difference made all the difference.

Early on, he said that if anyone looked confused or lost, he would "call [them] out on that." And he did. At one point, he asked a member of the audience to "just let me see how your brain is processing this information." The interaction gave him another chance to show his passion for the material and his true desire for all of us to "get it."

Passion is what's missing most from the presentations we all attend. As TJ Walker says, "Many presenters are so worried about making a bad impression that instead they make *no* impression." Express yourself with passion, and prepare enough to go "unplugged" when you have to.

A winning combination is simple: three Ps (Presence, Preparation, and Passion) multiplied by three Vs (Verbal, Vocal, and Visual).

You will have a 9-times better G.R.I.P. on your next presentation.

6

Three Solutions for "But This Topic Is Boring!" (Edited and updated version of chapter 31 from Get a G.R.I.P.)

Often, my clients find themselves at a loss even before they begin preparation. "I know it's important to convey conviction in my presentations," one project manager said, "so what can I do if they want me to talk about something I'm not interested in myself? How can I still dazzle the audience?"

Great question. After all, nothing puts an audience to sleep faster than a speaker who is bored himself or herself. So here are three specific ways to get the passion you need for the topic at hand.

. . .

1. Find the Right Person

HAVE you ever thought to yourself, "I don't care that much about [topic X]"? You say the topic bores you to death, yet you're supposed to wow your audience. Is it really the *topic* that is inherently boring, or is it just *your experience* with the topic? I bet there is *some*one who loves the topic you are supposed to speak about. In fact, there may be a whole discipline on it, whether your topic is supply chain logistics, internet marketing, cost reduction, project management, or just about anything else. Find someone who believes your topic is very interesting. Interview that person. Play detective and search until you find out why they're so passionate about it.

You'll then be able to start your next speech with something like, "I used to think logistics was the most boring subject in the world. Then I met Midori Suzuki, who set me straight. She showed me exactly how logistics has been the key to so many corporate successes, including world leaders like Nike, Toyota, and 7-11. What I have to share with you today may change forever how you view logistics."

2. Find the Connection

. . .

ANOTHER TRICK TO help jumpstart your thinking is to find the connection between your assigned topic and something you really *are* passionate about. Then you can use that subject as a metaphor and reshape your presentation around it. A client was asked to present on Network Security, something he's familiar with but not passionate about. An avid student of war history, he found the passion he was looking for by setting up his presentation in a new way, linking Network Security to successful war strategies.

You can do this with any topic. Remember the second "C" in the Heath brother's S.U.C.C.E.S. formula? It stands for "Concrete." One of my favorite training exercises is called "Everything is like everything else." We draw a vertical line on a whiteboard or sheet of paper, dividing the writing surface into a left and right side. On the left side, write down a few abstract nouns that your topic covers: logistics, projects, or marketing, for example. Then on the right side, list several concrete nouns. The nouns can be anything concrete, but work especially well when they're something you may be passionate about. They could be your favorite koa wood mini Taylor guitar or a new golf driver. Any real *thing* will do.

Then all you need is a little imagination, and you can turn a "dull" topic into something special–you just need to find the connection, a metaphor.

Remember to choose a metaphor that your audience can also relate to. Don't talk to a group of call center operators from Mumbai about baseball, or share *sumo* wrestling strategies with their Irish counterparts.

One metaphor that I still remember, and still makes me chuckle, was delivered by a group presenting to senior management of a famous beverage company, many years ago.

"Gentlemen," the presenter began, "our strategy has been like underwear. Changing every day."

3. Find the Questions

WHAT IF YOU can't find a good metaphor? Then try this: Empathize with your audience and find out what they want you to answer for them.

As a professional presenter, you'll be interesting when you're engaged in a sincere dialogue with your audience. Go through your content using no more than half of your allotted time, and get to the Question and Answer session. Prepare just as much or more for the Q & A as you do for your presentation. Also, be sure to let the audience know you're serious about taking their questions. Don't make the common mistake of rushing right past them with, "I guess there are no questions, so to sum up ..." Or worse, "No questions at this point? Good. I'll move on to...." When you say "good," you're signaling that it is "good" for there to be no questions.

And another piece of sound advice I wish I'd known 20 years ago: Finish your presentation with your prepared conclusion, after the Q & A, because you never know what kind of questions you're going to get. To leave a strong impression, finish answering as many questions as time allows, and then end with your own, well-prepared last line.

The Ultimate Connection

If none of the above seems to work for you, here's one more suggestion that just might do the trick: Remember your ultimate goal.

Almost no one likes to work out with weights or run the track simply to lift heavy iron objects or jog around in circles. But we all want the results from exercise. Next time you're given a topic you don't feel passionate about, you can motivate yourself by remembering why you're doing it in the first place. Professional experience? Paying for your kids' education? Find *that* reason and you may surprise yourself, and then your audience, with your newly found passion. Even for a topic as "dull as dishwater." Like logistics?

7

"Who you are speaks so loudly I can't hear what you're saying."
-- Ralph Waldo Emerson

What about the Q & A?

If audience members have prepared themselves to attend your presentation, they're curious about your topic. They arrive with some questions, whether prepared or not to ask. When you receive a question from the audience, that's the one moment you know beyond any doubt that what you're going to say next has at least one person's interest. That's why we "welcome" questions.

I love Jay Sullivan's section on dealing with questions in his book, *Simply Said*. I highly recommend the whole book and this part in particular. He shares the benefit of re-stating a question so as to buy time, gather your thoughts, etc. But he also cautions against using such a technique with an attack question like, "Isn't this just some kind of scam?" That's not the time to repeat the question, confirm what the speaker really wants to know, gather your thoughts, etc. No. That's the time to say, "No, it's not."

A great way to think about Q & A, and really, about any other interaction with people is to consider that every time you speak, you are "presenting." Avoid the pitfalls of "presentationality," that is, adopting some affectations (either speaking too softly, or with artificial gestures or showing off big vocabulary words), and just present yourself. You've heard "just be yourself" before. In this case, "be your best self." Follow the suggestions you've tested in this book. Review David Lambuth's *Little Book on Business Writing* and follow his seven Cs. Speak clearly. Practice. Yes, practice answering certain questions. And if no one asks the question, but it's a good one, ask it yourself, to yourself. "Many people ask..." or "You might ask...."

Give people time to absorb your content and to feel comfortable with you. By the way, if you want your audience to feel comfortable, you'll want to project comfort, not anxiety. There's a good TEDx Talk and many other sources you can turn to in order to reduce anxiety or what some call "stage fright." A simple re-framing works for me.

This is my inner dialog I go through before almost every public speaking engagement as I feel my heart pounding stronger than usual: I ask myself, "Why did I agree to do this...again?" I remind myself: "My heart is pounding because I have something important I want to share, and people are going to be paying attention to me. It's natural to feel nervous —or am I really nervous? Maybe I am just excited? Yes, that's it. I'm EXCITED!"

And I am excited. I'm excited for you to try out some or even just one of these or other techniques in your next presentation. I'm excited for you to deliver better presentations, and for you to help raise the level of presentations in your organization. This is truly "enlightened self-interest." I want you to succeed because I might be your coach, but I also might be in the audience, and I want to enjoy it.

QUESTIONS AND ANSWERS

A few readers of the pre-publication and first edition of *Get a G.R.I.P. on Presentations* already responded to my request for questions, so Enlightening Press brings you this "Edition 1A."

The first was asked by too many to mention, and since I addressed it in a recent blog post, I'm tackling it here.

The second came from Darren McKellin, Area Director, North Asia, for ZScaler.

If you have a question or topic you would like me to explore further, e-mail andrew@amt-group.com. Your questions, with your permission, may find their way into future editions of *Get a G.R.I.P. on Presentations*.

. . .

Q: I heard it's good to start off my presentation with a joke. What do you think?

A: Short answer: You're probably not funny enough to pull it off. The longer answer, taken from a recent blog post I wrote titled "Not Funny," is edited and expanded here:

AT ONE OF the first presentations I attended here in Japan, now more than 25 years ago, the presenter began: "Most Japanese speakers open with an apology, and many Western speakers open with a joke. So, I'll start by saying, 'I'm sorry I don't have a good joke to tell.'"

Many of us chuckled. A few months later, another speaker at a similar event tried the same introduction and received only groans from the audience. Here's the truth: Unless you're a professional comic, you're probably not funny enough to tell a joke at the start of your presentation. Oh, you can tell it, but you won't get the result you want. And what is that result, anyway?

Did you want the audience to think you're funny? Why? They didn't come to your talk for the laughs, did they? The reason (I hope) you're even thinking of telling a joke at the start of your presentation is to generate audience connection. And that's great. Westerners, according to *Polite Fictions*, by Nancy Sakamoto, live under the fiction that "You and I are equal." And what says "equal" more accurately or quickly than laughing at the same joke? So your heart's in the right place.

Japanese operate with different polite fictions. In Japanese, very often the best thing to say is nothing at all. A polite audience wouldn't want to make a lot of noise, such as laughing out loud, especially at a business presentation. So telling a joke at the start of a presentation to a Japanese (or most any "serious") audience will likely generate nothing but silence.

Again, the hard truth, repeated to help it sink in: You're probably not that funny. If you're the boss, you may be accustomed to people laughing at your jokes. But they're laughing because you're the boss, not because what you said is funny.

A story I heard, that may or may not be true, makes the above point. It seems that former U.S. President Jimmy Carter once spoke to the Japanese Diet (Congress), using an interpreter. He began with a joke, and was pleased at the audience response, since he wasn't sure if his humor would carry across the Pacific. After the speech, he complimented his interpreter, who said, "Oh, I didn't translate your joke. I told them that the President of the United States just told a joke, so please laugh."

Ninety percent of the time when I share that story with an audience, I get quite a bit of laughter.

But note that it's *not* a joke, and though I told you that you're not funny, I'll admit it here: I'm not funny either. At least not "professional" funny. Nobody has paid me to make them laugh. Unless you've been paid to make people laugh, my advice is simple: Stay away from jokes.

I learned this the "hard way" a couple of years ago, while spending a weekend with Kevin Ruf, class president (and class clown) from my high school. In the ensuing years since graduation, Kevin became an attorney and simultaneously a member of the Groundlings. This West Coast version of the Second City, Groundlings members are comedians who often go on to their own TV shows (as Kevin did, with *Halfway Home* on HBO) or to roles on *Saturday Night Live* and other comedies. It takes years to get into the Groundlings, and it took me less than a weekend to recognize the grand gulf between people who think they are funny and a professional comedian.

Stand-up comics are masters of the Verbal, Vocal, and Visual delivery of their material. They test their approach with different audiences, and they've received all kinds of feed-back well before you or I see them live or on YouTube or a Netflix special. Those who can improvise in the moment, like Kevin, often get paid to *teach* improvisation. They are really, really good. And yet their jokes sometimes "bomb," meaning even these pros don't always get the laughs they hoped for. Are you comfortable "bombing" at the start of your presentation? Nothing destroys confidence quicker.

This is not to say, "Give up!" Go ahead and share your sense of humor. Be self-deprecating. Put up the occasional, universally funny slide or short video clip, but remember your objective. Or better still, remember your audience's objective. Did they come to see you for laughs? No. If you remember to focus on their objectives, you're much more likely to hit yours.

Q: What about the presenter who, when in front of a group, just starts speaking before getting the audience's attention? Can you address that? — Darren McKellin, Area Director, North Asia, ZScaler.

A: An excellent question from Darren, who has spoken in front of hundreds of audiences over his 20+ years as a leader in the American Chamber of Commerce in Japan. Short answer: "Don't do that!"

THE LONGER ANSWER:

. . .

ONE OF THE advanced skills to master as a public speaker is the use of silence. In chapter 2, we covered pausing as the "killer vocal tool." Standing in front of an audience and saying nothing can enhance your presence, your gravitas. If people are talking, and you just start talking above them, sometimes the audience will quiet down, but other times you may never get their full attention, and even if you eventually do, a lot of people will have missed your opening.

Years ago I used the "Shhhh" method. People do tend to quiet down when they hear "Shhhh," since most everyone's mother soothed us with that calming sound. But there are a couple of problems with this method:

1) Some will complain they are being treated as babies.

2) Jerry Seinfeld once said something like, "I don't want to be a "shusher." I prefer being a shushee."

Hence, I've put my "Shhh" on the shelf, and these days only rarely take it down.

Another method I dislike is tapping a wine or water glass with a knife. First, you might break the glass. Second, it's an unpleasant, jarring sound. And third, you're not a bell-ringer, you're the invited speaker.

It's best if the person introducing you quiets the crowd. That way, when you're ready to speak, the room is ready for you. But what if the audience isn't ready? Give them at least a minute, or maybe two. Just stand, grounded, breathing deeply, exhaling fully, smiling, acknowledging with a positive nod, perhaps a wave, those who *are* paying attention to you. If, after two full minutes (which may feel like an eternity until you're comfortable with this technique), you still don't have their attention, say, "Ladies and Gentlemen."

That's really all you need to say. If they're still not paying attention 30 seconds later, say, slowly, purposefully, "Ladies and Gentlemen, please." (If it helps, imagine you're the chair umpire at Wimbledon.) You might need to say it one more time. Then, "Thank you."

Now, only now, with the audience's full attention, is the time to launch your presentation.

Got a question? Email: andrew@amt-group.com

References

Jay Sullivan, *Say It Simple*

David Peoples, *Presentations Plus*

Timothy Gallwey, *The Inner Game of Tennis* and *Inner Tennis: Playing the Game*

Andrew W. Silberman, *Get A G.R.I.P.: 15 Minutes a Day to Greater Global Readiness®*

YouTube videos:

Susan Weinschenk, *5 Things Every Presenter Needs to Know About People*

Allan Pease, Body Language: *The Power is in the Palm of Your Hands*

IF YOU ENJOYED THIS BOOK...

If you enjoyed this book, please consider subscribing to our mailing list at www.amt-group.com. Reviews are great assistance. If you liked the book, please consider leaving your thoughts in the review section of the online retailer where you made the purchase.

ABOUT THE AUTHOR

Andrew Silberman has been inspiring improvement in individuals and organizations since 1989. At AMT Group, which he co-founded in Tokyo in 1992, he leads a multi-national team of facilitators and administrative staff whose mission is: *Developing Global Thinkers*.

Andrew was born in Chicago, Illinois, and lived his primary through high school years in Saratoga, California. He holds a bachelor's degree in the Political Economy of Industrial Societies from U.C. Berkeley and graduated (with distinction) with an MBA in international management from the Fisher School of Business at the Monterey Institute of International Studies.

www.ingramcontent.com/pod-product-compliance
Lightning Source LLC
Chambersburg PA
CBHW070812220526
45466CB00002B/645